Perhaps Life!

Aliveni Arrala

BookLeaf Publishing

India | USA | UK

Presentation by *BookLeaf Publishing*

Web: www.bookleafpub.com

E-mail: info@bookleafpub.com

ISBN: 9789363314498

First edition 2024

Perhaps Solace!

As the green waves comes nearby welcomes,

The breeze of air that mildly touches my hair as
it comes,

The sunshines that kisses my cheek,

The droplets of water that sprinkles on my face,

The smell of freshness is what I sense that
inflates my lungs as I inhale,

What is this beauty my breath holds and asks do
I exhale?

Going out of balance as I stand on this boat,

However this stillness perfectly balances my
soul.

I stand here and stare at you all along,

The breeze that comes and hugs me strongly and
tightly as I am not here for forever long.

There is a lot of noise I see but can only hear
your rhythm, the perfect green sea.

I will never forget the solace you gave me in a
few seconds,

I will carry that with me as a small part of me as
I go wherever!
@Venice, Italy

Perhaps Sometimes!

Sometimes everything in you cries except your eyes,

Making it extremely hard to remain calm and wise.

Would it happen with everyone around,

Well it might, it's karma, what goes around comes around.

The bundle of lies heard, that are just around the mind,

Why just not get rid and throw them all into the wind,

It feels weird when surrounded by people, where no one understands,

It's stagnant as hell where I currently stand.

It's harder for a moment to pass, as I make it unworthy,

The more the time passes, the more I am afraid,
I am far from earthy.

Call it halt or call it stall whatever, my mind just
stops in this season,

Am I searching for light in dark places for the
wrong reason?

Eventually it's totally getting hard to realize and
pause and read the correct clause.

Would there be light at the end of the tunnel?

Thoughts are dripping without control just like
in a funnel.

May be sometimes when you are in a dark place,
you think I have been buried,

And you would be worried,

May be in actual you might have been planted,

Now all I need is to grow and bloom which is all
I wanted.

Perhaps start over it says!

Sometimes you give up on yourself, lose
yourself, break yourself apart into pieces,

Maybe often you are your own creator of your
crisis.

It may feel, there is no strength to pull the pieces
to fix,

Because everything around, just seems jinxed.

But what if a new life is waiting and you are still
sitting and taunting,

What if the best days are yet to start,

What if this heartbreak is a foundation for
another level of life to restart.

What if the excitement is yet to begin and burst,

To realize the worth of the best, you have been
through the worst.

Maybe it's never too late unless you think it that
ways,

Maybe you have to fight through some bad days to earn life's best days.

Remember you can never be enough for everyone but for yourself even when you don't understand it,

Do you even realize, you will never speak to anyone more than you speak to yourself in your head, better be kind to yourself and feel it.

At the end, the point is why should you even be afraid to start over again?

You never know, you may like your new story better!

Your new story could be your favorite and hitter!

Perhaps eyes speak?

As the strong breeze sharpens and flows,

Just getting frozen in the cold as I walk on these roads and the way things goes.

It's a daily activity for me to pick the fallen leaves,

Wondering and wishing they would stick forever to the branches and lives.

As the days pass by this way, amidst these usual ritual,

I had a surreal encounter that really left me with thought residual

As you walk towards me in blue, my mind has it still recorded,

I wonder if it is for real, because none of it seems distorted.

Let's think this way, it's an enforced custom for me to never give an eyesight,

But then unconsciously this one time I still did
fall into the bite.

That moment when my eyes fell into the well of
your eyes,

It was a rare feeling of Lost and I quite
remember it as nice.

However till this minute it surprises me, what I
saw in your eyes!

That moment I was scared, as your eyes were
screaming uncertainty/instability,

For once it was a sudden pull of getting lost in
them for eternity.

It might be just my delusion,

I don't want to say it out loud nor agree or create
myself a not needed illusion.

Few days later, you told me about your
heartbreak,

Maybe there were certain frustrations and fears,
your life might not be a walk on the cake.

Am I still bewildered, because you conveyed
sadness, you conveyed disappointment,

As I traveled along, I understood you might be
alone, struggling with immense grief in heart,

And so many mixed emotions on your chart.

But why could not see any of these? I saw it,
like you can't stand in this place not that place,

Nor this side, neither that side, you can't stand in
one place grounded but running.

Just like an unstable element in the periodic
table gunning!

Many times, I thought I would share this with
you, but this question stops me. What if I am
wrong and it's just a wrong read and feeble?

You looked perfectly fine on the outside,
everything under control and nothing seemed
dreadful.

May be I am afraid of your rage, even though I
want to know if this is true or false but would
never dare to confront,

Like every time words keep buzzing in my
mind, but I am too afraid of you and cannot put
a word in front!

Eventually I figured out, the best way is to stop
looking into your eyes,

Because uncertainty scares me to hell and time
always flies.

I still wish I read you wrong!

I don't know why I am so insensitive, regardless,
I wish I could have patted your back to hug and
told you take one day at a time. And This too
shall pass just go along.

I wish I could tell you slowly is the fastest way
to get to where you want to be!

And I believe someday you would definitely
conquer the sea!

Perhaps pick a Side!

The petals of flowers that outburst as a laughter,

The distant dreams that are to dissolve and
scatter.

Should I hold them back or let them lose to flow,

Maybe let them flow and set them free and glow.

The sun and moon never meet yet so
synchronous and quite,

Maybe they wait for an eclipse to occur without
complaint.

There are two sides of a story always,

The heard one makes noise, while the unheard
part stands crossways.

Why do I always pick the other side of the
story?

Maybe others listen to reply but I always listen
to understand that's why!

Perhaps No Rush!

Why do you always run, and from what are you running away,

Take a pause, hold your breath for a second, halt your thought, look away.

There is no need of such an adrenaline rush,

Just be entitled, there is no need to bother yourself much.

Do you even realize, and compose yourself from noise,

And filter away the nuisance to enjoy little joys.

Realize there is nothing you can really change or create,

There is already a lot of fuss, delete it without a thought just straight.

Don't get annoyed with small little tempers, the world is there for that purpose.

Build a wall in your mind, just don't be affected
by this circus.

Disappointments are part and parcel of life, life
is insane,

Just wear an invisible armor and say, try me yet
again.

You would win some day, maybe not
immediately but definitely.

Be in conscience that you worked it so far strong
and brilliantly.

I notice even the small gesture you do and say,

Could you just halt and hear me? I said so much
in silence, but you didn't listen and had no time
to pay!

Perhaps lost!

Lost in the direction in which my heart wants to go,

It asks me, something unheard, something unseen, what exactly do you want to know?

It says "you have already traveled in this direction a long way".

Would you want to stop, take a turn and get away?

Somethings hidden so deep in the dark, I am afraid to sustain,

Even if I find them, I fall short of words to explain.

May be I can clearly see you standing there on the distant river bank,

My heart wants to come there, but something in me stops and fears it might be not you but just a sham!

I know, I can see and sense it clearly, my heart
just screams,

Would I have come if not tied with unseen
strings?

Do I wish to find a way, this might be the road I
should take?

Searching for some direction, or may be I am
already there not realizing,

Maybe you have taken me away unknowingly
on this road already a long way.

Perhaps The perfect distraction!

Cloning all the ways trying to recollect,

Floating through the waves fearing to disconnect.

All the sunshines which pass through me screams,

The rays that would reflect and slip into dreams.

For all the detached leaves that fall on the ground,

Seems like a perfect welcome while I walk around.

Sooner or later, I would come out of this dream,

Just to realize, what does it even mean?

Twinkles and winkles of happy feels you give,

I hope I can always rewind them and relive.

This is too perfect to call it an unrealistic dream,

That's why I call it a perfect distraction to
redeem!

Perhaps Vicinity!

It just surprises me and I wonder why I don't feel
lonely even when I am alone,

I don't feel a need to be surrounded, has my
heart become stone?

There is no urge to be around people,

Indeed, I am starting to feel alone when I am
with them.

Let me goof around myself, this way I can't get
hurt,

Calm and composed, just being with myself on
this earth.

Traveling across as I sit near the window,

And just quietly observe the movement of my
shadow.

I see no one in my near vicinity.

There is absolutely nothing that gets to my
proximity!

Perhaps Let's win together or lose together!

When there is always a need to win,

Remember, you may have won an argument, but you may have lost me a bit.

Trying to figure out why is that push for people wanting to be right?

Why don't you cut down your ego and see it through straight?

When you are caught up in a high ride of emotion,

Just come to consciousness and watch around. Do you feel any sensation?

May be sometimes agree to disagree with yourself,

Because, just remember, "In the war of egos, the winner is the biggest loser."

Perhaps it's Rain!

A beautiful Sunday, as I open my window and look through,

These tiny little droplets caught my attention from which I cannot withdraw!

The stems and the leaves that are drenching in rain,

Observing me, as I look at them with eyes filled with vain!

The green grass looked cheerful as they get immersed in the wet sprinkle,

Perhaps I can gaze at it for hours straight,

Of course green is indeed my favorite!

But, this gives my soul a lot of peace and solace,

Just gazing at it being flawless!

I wish I could join you and drench in rain,

And let my fright and fear drain!

Perhaps Indelible!

The hopeful sunrises, the brave sunsets,

Colorful days, the peaceful nights,

Green bright leaves, the dancing winds,

Shining stars, the snow-white moon,

Smile on lips, blush on the cheeks,

Curly hair, the random acts of glare,

Mischief of wink, gaze of the eyes,

Warmth of the vicinity, and all the affinity,

As close as zero, and as true as the infinity,

More in dreams, far from the reality,

No's from mind, Yes's from the heart,

Perhaps my memory etched you,

More than ephemeral I have known you!

Perhaps Wonder or Thunder?

As I Just sit and think about you,

It makes me question, am I the only one going
through this or do you?

I see a field full of green leaves however,

The weeds just have grown strongly in weaves.

Should I safeguard the greens or

cut through the weeds?

Which one to pick, both look exhaustive,

Here I stand crossways without being intuitive.

The creepers are spread across with strong
strings,

However the bushes are branched out with
Infinite springs,

Which one to choose, both look tedious,

Here I see both ways, as I look at one, and tend
to forget the previous.

The river that flows across the stream,

And the fall that never stops and flows extreme,

Here I stand on land and feeling the thunder,

In which water should I immerse myself as I
wonder!

Perhaps Bewildered!

The converging edge you are now to held,

The verge of actions that just get repelled.

The beams of particles you can only see,

The linings of the cloud which always flee.

Could be, the corona of the eyes that gets much red deepened,

Soon the thought of my sight awakened.

Finding charismatic ways to get you a thought,

Wait! It's always and ever a storm soon to be caught.

Ambitioning to get cloned as one is not abundant,

Tear down the scars of exhaustion which is only redundant!

Perhaps in quest of Happiness!

In quest of happiness,

Every time I take a step to search for happiness in something,

The outcome was nothing!

I just come back a few steps back to myself and realize,

The only one whom I can be happy with is myself!

Close to water, close to moon, close to dark, close to light,

But no wonder I found an answer for my fight.

Hold my breath, stopped my thoughts, ran my tears, pinch myself,

But where is the truth? Nowhere I can't find the truth itself.

No one can even dare to go, and let it go,

Happiness is something to live within as we grow!

Perhaps the Sunshines!

27

The sun that shines in the morning,

The birds that are always in joy humming!

Sitting on the edge thinking will I ever make it happening,

The dreams that you have been dreaming,

Knowing through reality and realizing,

Pause a moment for yourself empathizing,

Because you are really worthy and deserving!

Perhaps it happens

It happens, it changes, it molds,

Finally it helps, it soothes,

It happens in life, at times,

It happens in life, one day,

It happens in life, for months,

It happens in life, for a moment may be,

It happens, it teaches you,

It happens, it enriches you,

It happens, it shows you that you are better now
and can be the best tomorrow,

It happens, you fail one day,

It happens, that failures may help you win the
rest of every days,

It happens, it puts you in line,

It happens, it sorts,

It happens...it happens finally it completes the
picture of your life,

which includes all the colors without which it's
incomplete and makes your life a colorful

and a complete canvas.

So always be thankful that it happens (had
happened)

Instead of thinking about why it happens (had
happened)

If you still think in the same way, that's fine
because it happens!

Perhaps My great brain!

The canopy of thoughts spread across the neurons,

Have I settled them upon, just bring on!

Do I hallucinate these disappearing thoughts,

Absolutely not, as they are still stuck caught!

Are you even for real, questions my medulla oblongata,

Sense everything, it pricks says amygdala!

Dendrite after dendrite curses every single thought,

As the terabytes of data that gets processed oft!

It's just garbage says my brain,

I agree to disagree, says my heart.

Perhaps the Road not taken!

For all those years I kept you far away,

I have realized I have driven myself that way!

Engulfing the moments of the real,

Could not believe they seemed so surreal!

Varied people, varied souls with utmost varied goals,

We are miles apart and too distant it feels!

Sometimes it's hard to forget the road not taken,

But in the end it's worth it for the decisions foretaken!

Perhaps Life is like sailing!

May be to own my life is to own my wounds,

Let the scars shine and bright and grow with them with no bounds.

Let the blood flow deeply and freely through the veins with speed,

That there is no stagnancy in my body that halts a need.

I feel pain everywhere, to get rid of it, I am needy,

I remember someone said, pain is just a weakness leaving the body.

Evolve in the universe as there is no limit,

Smiling away at the obstacles and savoring every minute.

Gather the strength inside you and see the light,

Let the breath behold and just don't stop your fight.

Nothing is precious than a room of your own,

Safe place where the soul blossoms and habits are grown.

Well, what option you have apart from setting yourself to sail,

All you have is an unending ocean to avail!

Perhaps a word that describes your Life?

A bit by bit as we close down our chapter,

The more we feel, we should have filled it with laughter.

The cons are always there as a custom,

But the pros are always hidden underneath accustomed..

The more moments we live and take life for granted,

Just running behind the so-called things we wanted.

Grown in age, grown in person, better to remain in somethings ingrown,

Keep the child in you always intact and unflown.

They say life is all about living differently,

But if you only follow convention, expect it to
be only conventionally.

The world is all about living with the
acquaintances,

The more you learn them, the more it intimidates
your senses.

If asked a word to summarize your life,

What would it be? and what would you want it
to be?

Perhaps in Celebration of being alive!

The petals that shade away from the bloom,

The stem that stands alone in gloom!

Aren't they really aware of this disjunction,

But still stick together with such compassion!

Since forever is also not forever,

Let's not think about it any time ever,

They say, now is the time we stick together,

Let's not leave any moment to gather!

This thought makes me feel alive,

Let's not be any other person but to be naive!

In the end, this is something to believe and
thrive,
In celebration of being alive!

www.ingramcontent.com/pod-product-compliance
Lightning Source LLC
Chambersburg PA
CBHW071236140726
47996CB00007B/2631